EDEN-FARMS

Eden-Farms

A Cooperative Organic Style Farm Community

Kerry Freeman
co-author Robbin Rivka Freeman

To order additional copies of this book, contact:
Xlibris
1-888-795-4274
www.Xlibris.com
Orders@Xlibris.com
803327

Disclaimer

All of the ideas about community development for people interested in organic farming and eating plantbased are the product of the thoughts of Kerry Freeman. We realize there may be better ideas to be researched and utilized, so other concepts or improvements are welcome.

The following is an outline for community housing development featuring organic farming, growing food and amenities that facilitate whole food plantbased living. The idea is to create a total organic farm to plan and grow totally pure organic vegetables for those strict people that believe and require pure grown products. There is a great need and movement in the world for soil regeneration and growing plantbased whole foods for a healthier lifestyle, to contribute to saving the climate and the environment, and to give the animals a break.

All of the ideas are a suggestion for operations. Suggestions are welcome; plans can be changed or improved upon. There is always some person that can find a different way to enhance the plan, in part or even the entire project. I would be glad to discuss the subject of any changes, with any interested party. I can be reached at <u>mrkings@aol.com</u>.

Kerry Freeman

Eden Farms is a housing development centered around community and growing fresh local organic food for personal consumption, for bartering with neighbors and for selling locally grown organic produce.

Why create a community housing development featuring organic farming?

Consumers want to eat food that contributes to health and wellbeing; whole plant foods that enable us to resist disease and maladies common in 2019.

Consumers want to eat plant foods in order to use less environmental resources, in order to use less water and create less waste. People want to reduce their exposure to environmental toxins like pesticides, herbicides, metals, neurotoxins and endocrine disrupting substances. Consumers want to minimize second hand exposure to antibiotics and medications that are given to animals grown for food.

People want to increase food security by growing their own

food; having a plot of land for growing food or being a member of a community green house or farming community; or having access to purchase locally grown, seasonal, organic, non GMO whole food plant based produce with the seeds intact is a high priority.

Farming provides jobs and sustainability both economically and environmentally. Security for people means creating a way to spend less money and have better quality fresher food to eat.

The village or community style housing for families and dormitory apartment style housing for unattached persons will be available; all residents will ideally be able to participate in growing whole plant food for consumption purposes, for sustenance, within the community development.

My father relishes the community development lifestyle where he lives in Florida. There's a community for everything you could possibly be into, golfing, swimming, tennis, drama, dance, gaming. In Florida about every other mile is another housing community. He has always wanted me to move to Florida so he thought of this idea of a housing development with organic farming because he knows how important eating organic whole plant foods is to me. He never stops trying to make things happen. However, he thinks like a rich person who doesn't move that much. I am imagining Eden Farms as a community where you can plant your own food and spend a lot of time outdoors, and always have access to whole plant foods that are fresher and less expensive than buying produce in the store. I want to work on planting and getting exercise by working on my garden.

Ideally plots of land should be available for those who want to do their own gardening to grow food and plots should be available for those who want to pay a fee for fresh local food to be grown in the community.

Cooperative Dimensions

The ideal area dimension would be 2 miles wide and ("east to west"). And 2 miles long. ("south to north").

In the absence of ideal, the minimum area size as described in this proposal, would be 10,000 feet wide and 8000 feet long, this would provide enough land area to build the support living and processing areas and the fields in which to grow our products.

Basically, the east and west sides of property area would be the growing fields. Four of them, each 4000 feet wide by 3000 feet long. The residential and commercial areas, would be in the center in an area of approximately 900 feet wide and 800 feet long. These general areas, would be broken into at least 4 parts.

<u>Southern area</u> would be commercial retail section housing the stores and service areas need for the cooperative population to have goods and services for them live on and perform their daily functions. <u>Northern area</u> would be cooperative functions, such a packing shipping, municipal operations, cooperative operations and utility functions.

East and west sides would be residential and recreational areas, to provide housing, educational and recreational functions, needed for normal living. It is most important, that adequate housing be available, for the employees and workers of the cooperative. This creates loyalty and in willingness to work within the cooperative.

The areas for farming are approximately 30 acres each field. Objectively, the overall area will be divided into 4 sections of farmland set in a quadrangle 3000 x 4000 feet each section. Center of the sections would ideally be bisected by a lake or a river to create an irrigation system, each ficld will try to plant two crops per year, spring and fall, if possible. A basic crew to tend crops as they are growing will live on or near each section for seeding and picking times, transient workers can be hired and housed on cooperative. Each farm will be operated by a different group or owner, and then cooperate in packaging and shipping. Other organic farm project can be developed in the immediate area. At each end of the fields a commercial area would be created such as Front St, at one end that would house the packing and warehousing buildings and all other offices and service facilities along with medical and other civic functions - such as fire control and peacekeeping at the other end would be Main St.; providing all the retail outlets - such as a power market, gas station, bank, and all the usual service stores each enterprise would be individually run and operated, for individual profit, employing their own crews.

ATLANTIC AVE

400   500   510   300   650   250   400

GRAND AVE

LITTLE FOLKS INN   LONGVIEW COND   VISTA ROOM   RECREATION HOUSING   ATELIER ROOM   COMMERCIAL OPERATIONS   FRONT ST

WATER WAY

410   460   350   600   650   250   400

GRAND AVE

HESS MALL   TENNIS COURT / BASKET BALL / WEAVERS   BALLFIELD   RESTAURANTS   COURTHOUSE SERVICES   FRONT ST

CHUN AVE   TENNIS CT   RESIDENTIAL HOUSING

PACIFIC AVE

N

Board of Directors

General Manager <u>or</u> Asst - President of Board

Clerical Department Manager - Daily Operations

Accounting Department Manager - Finances-Payroll etc.

Human Resources Manager - Hiring - Personnel Problems

Real Estate and Property Mgr Collect Rents and Distribution

Packaging and Distribution Mgr - Prepare and Ship Products

Field Operations Mgr - Coordinate Fields and Usage

Workers Services Mgr - Dorms - Managing Activities

Resident Services Mgr - Security - Transportation etc

South Section - Retail Stores and Services

North Section Operational and Productive Services

North West Section - Partial Residential and Services

North East Section Partial Residential and Services

South West Section Partial Residential and Services

South East Section Partial Residential and Services

Board of Directors Consists of 15 persons either

Appointed by Job Position or Residents Election.

Project will Represent - The best interest of all residents and

working personnel and act in their best interest

A Quarter will consist of 9 or more representatives.

A vote approval will be a majority 1 - or more

The board will act without any personal compensation

Valid expenses may be approved by the board president

One clerical person will act as secretary and scribe recording procedures and subject activities

1 hr. base pay allotted for after hours participation in quarterly meeting or any emergency meeting

Eden Farms - An organic grower cooperative

(1)The basic idea is to create a space for each family or individual to do their own organic farming, choosing vegetables, fruits, herbs, sprouts they want to grow. Seasonal varieties can be grown according to the climate and zone map for any area all year long. Any root vegetable can be harvested in winter like beets and potatoes; that's why Russians love beets and potatoes. There are appropriate plants for every season. The development could feature a community green house; or families or individuals could purchase a plot of land adjacent to your townhouse, or home; and have a full or partial temperature controlled green house, in order to grow produce you desire, all year long.

This is where my father and I differ in opinion. I imagine this utopian community as a place where I can grow what I like in my backyard and I could barter food with neighbors and always be able to pick and eat the healthiest greens, freshly picked. I believe there are many people who would like to be able to move into a community where you buy the house and the land to farm because you want to participate in choosing what to grow and eat. Jobs for teenagers and young adults in the family would be available; and the community assists you to live the plantbased lifestyle.

I don't imagine the community as my Dad does, a rich person's community where there is hired help doing everything. The younger generation don't have money socked away to spend on hired help. There are many people who would benefit from a sustainable food growing lifestyle where you replant seeds and rotate your square foot garden crops according to what is seasonal, what you like and what will work with the weather; in order to have a supply of healthy food that costs very little to grow and maintain. I guess there could be a variety of organic farming communities where some communities allow the residents to chip in for the upkeep of the green house and community garden for folks who don't want to get their hands dirty but want to eat whole food plantbased freshly grown.

(2) Most important is the personel needed to operate this cooperative. Not only do we need field workers on a permanent basis, to work and tend the fields, but we also need transient workers during the planting and picking seasons. We also need workers to operate the service facilities in preparing the product

for shipment, not to mention the people needed to provide simple life sustaining services, we also need people to work in the retail stores, that provide the basic needs of the community population.

While the majority of the people working and providing the overall different services will be minimum or lower wage category, we will still need some skilled and qualified people to supervise or operate or even oversee all the people and offices and equipment.

All of there people who will most probably constitute an entire community, most have housing provided for them, that they can afford on what ever pay level they may be at any however many their family consists of. This is being mentioned because lower income people, tend to have more children who need care and education.

Therefor we, must also provide schools which meet state standards and obtain and house their teachers also. It may be possible to enlist U.I.S.T.A. to join us in providing there services.

Operational Personel

General Manager - The buck stops here

Asst G.M. for any assistance of G.M.

Operational Clerks 3/1 Mgr and 2 Assistants

Accounting Clerks 3/1 Mgr and 2 Assistants

Operational - Take care of daily operations as needed

Accounting - Payroll - Income - Bills - cash flow etc.

Humans Resources 3/1 Mgr AM 2 Assistants

Interview and submit new hires - Subject to upper management approval as needed

Handle Insurance - Bonuses and General Personel

Section Representative - Elected - now compensated

Except for approved expenses - representing the public

Board of Directors - Elected Section Representatives along with managers of each department and upper management. G.M. will preside - meeting every 3 months required, unless called sooner by GM

Any expenditure over $5000 must be approved by the board on a majority basis

Profit Sharing - 50% of net profit on an annual basis

After Audit. Will be distributed to stockholders

50% of net profit will be distributed to all permanent personel

Transient personel not included in profit sharing

Management Persons

Field Personel

Operational Persons

Service Persons

Production Distribution Persons - 1/5 of total net share to be distributed equally in each group

Transient Personel

Transient personel will only be utilized on special occasions, such as planting or picking (harvesting) or special emergencies and no other times.

During these special times, whereby additional temporary personel is needed -They will be housed in either mansions dormitory's or special 2 bedroom bungalows for people with family dependents.

These transients houses in the dormitory's the payroll will be $6 per hour including, housing and meals in transient mess hall. For transients with dependents - (Head of house hold only) living in a 2 bedroom bungalow (no more than 3 dependents) the payroll will be $7 per hour including housing. Meals not included and not available in the transient mess hall. All meals should be available at residence with dependent family at own expense less a 10% discount at community food stores, subsidized by cooperative using a discount card.

All other rules and facilities are available to transients at posted rates.

During non-transients seasons the transient facility's will be closed and non-operative

Personnel to operate transient facilities will be recruited from among the transients.

Field personel need 12 per field or 1/8 total dormitory personel for meal service any housekeeping to be determined.

Working Force and Personel

32 <u>Field Workers</u> - 8 men per quarter sections, 4 to a half section on a permanent year round care-taking total 32 workers payroll amount, will be $9.00 per hour or minimum wage plus subsidies and bonuses for all employees.

2 <u>Foreman</u> to a double section east side west side total 2 men with a 10% increase in base pay hours will be 8:30 am to 5:00 pm or 8 hours per day 6 days per week. Total 50 hours base time and pay lunch break ½ hour between 11:30 am and 1:30 pm on a rotation basis. - Lunch will be in community mess hall rest breaks 15 minutes between 10 am and 11 am rotating basis and

3:00 pm and 4:00 pm. Casual supervision and bonus incentives for productive endeavor.

4 <u>Landscape and Community Maintenance</u> 4 person crew including supervisor - using the same work and pay schedule as the care for the community non farming areas, and roadways working on 1 of 6 areas each day.

1 <u>Specialty Personel</u> - <u>Irrigation</u> Controller - Caring for all waterways and sub stream areas. Inspecting the piping and watering heads, canals and flow. Utilize extra help from the field as needed. Same 6 day work schedule self-supervised - payroll $10 per hour 50 hour work week

1 <u>Community General Maintenance</u> Controller caring for minor repairs for non-farming community - (Handy man)

Inspect and repair central community. Same 6 day schedule and $10 per hour work week 50 hours

Generally there will be no work on Sunday except in emergency

<u>House Keepers and Dormitory</u> Maintenance.

There will be 2 housekeepers, maintaining the four resident dormitories - 2 north and 2 south. Providing basic cleaning and straightening services. Changing linens once per week and providing daily clean towel replacement, laundry service for linens and towel etc. Living conditions will be provided for each employee residents will make up their own beds and maintain areas.

<u>Cooks and Kitchen Personel</u>, for communication mess hall a crew of 8 will provide meals and maintain the community dining room (mess hall) planning meals for anticipated eating personel, any purchasing needed supplies to create, prepare, and serve the community at large, as needed. Meals are open to all, but not mandatory. Cost factor as follows

Monthly meal tickets 3 per day 7 per week $500.00

Weekly meal ticket 3 per day 7 per week $135.00

Meal ticket 2 meals day no lunch - <u>deduct</u> $4 per day

Daily meals breakfast $5 Lunch $7.50 dinner $11

<u>Additional Personel</u> maybe recruits on a part time basis. From dependent personel, compensation to be determined examined - housekeeping day work - Dog walking and babysitting office or store cleaning or even part time retail store clerking or office clerking.

<u>Sports Facilities</u> 2 tennis courts 2 basketball courts 2 handball courts and a full size football/soccer field & swimming pool and other facilities to be considered working force and personel

10 Employees for Packing plant and storage facilities and

all other non-<u>Field General Personel</u> same basic pay schedule - minimum wage or $9 per hour 50 hours per week 6 days per week

2 Supervisors - or foremen - Also on the same schedule and conditions - lunch included at community mess hall

Plus all subsidies - bonuses and incentives

Promotions and incentives - Always from within the ranks

<u>Services and Stores</u> will be individually owned and operated. All using their own work and pay schedules

<u>Professional Services</u> will also use their own schedules and pay programs - Specialty services - May share space and operate 1 or 2 days per week only on a schedule.

All employees and supervisors, will be offered housing on a subsidized and need basis

Single employees may utilize dormitory's @ $300 per mo

Family Groups - 2-4 dependents - 2 bedroom units

Free standing house @ $500 per mo - condo $450 per mo

3 bedroom units - 3-8 dependents. (4 children)

Free standing house @ $650 per mo condo $600 per mo

4 bedroom free standing house @ $1,000 per mo

6 to 8 dependents or 2 family's sharing

Meals available in community mess hall - 3 meals per day

Daily 3 meals - breakfast $3. - lunch, $7.50 dinner $11 per day Weekly ticket $135 monthly ticket $500 per person

Available to merchants and suppliers employee also other basic services provided by cooperative

<u>Security Officers</u> to provide observation and prevention security provide 7 days per week - Basic hours of 6 am to 11 pm, by a crew of 3. Rotating time in 9 hour shifts. No basic coverage needed between 12 am and 6 am, when most if not all are quiet and asleep. All are on duty in case of emergency, basic responsibility a-sense of observation and a presence of security over the community Officers will not be armed and in case of a real emergency, we will call 911 and the sheriff Officers will have the ability to issue citations for infractions of community rules and laws.

A voluntary court panel will convent once a month to hear appeals of any summons that are disputed.

<u>Transportation Drivers.</u> A 20 passenger will drive around community in a right handed circle to provide transportation with in the cooperative. Each rotation, should take about ½ hour, making 32 round trips per day. From 6:30 am to 10:30 pm daily except Sunday. 4 drivers are needed working 4 days on and 4 days off rotating time schedules fare cost will be by travel

card or 50¢ per trip, travel card will cost by trips $10 - 12 trips $5.00. Driver will punch fare card upon entering bus.

Bus will travel only in one direction, in a right turn route, circling the community. Drivers will maintain vehicles

Additional personel for support operations

Retail stores - Most service and supply outlets will offer hours of 10 am to 7 pm daily Monday to Saturday with later hours to 9 pm on Thursday and closed on Sunday

Some retail outlets may need to adjust their hours to suit their needs. Examples as follows. Breakfast/lunch diner 6 am to 3 pm dinner cafe 3 pm to 9 pm, newsstand 7 am to 8 pm, supermarket 8 am to 5 pm - theater noon to 9 pm bank - 9 am to 4 pm - truck stop 24 hours per day and so forth. This is an example of a small village each outlet will operate individually and rent space from the cooperative at reasonable rates on a net/net lease, paying all taxes and utilities etc.

The same goes for professional services such as doctors, lawyers, accountants, insurance agency etc except that they may share space and work on an alternating days basis. The expenses may be shared on a partnership basis. Hours generally on an 8 am to 4 pm basis 5 days per week - Monday to Friday closer Saturday and Sunday or by appointment.

Generally speaking the cooperative will own all the land,

and rent space to residents and other workers and all service and supply operators. Leases may be offered, but not needed, some property may resold on a cooperative basis. Subject to cooperative regular rules, and expenses, with limited title.

Front Street will be located at northern end of cooperative and will house the commercial needs of the cooperative.

<u>Northwest Corner</u> will provide an area for a truck stop, which will service the trucks needed to transport the produce grown at the cooperative to all the points of distribution that will dispense all our goods as part of this truck stop will be a fueling station which will dispense gasoline and diesel fuel in addition to recharging stations for hybrid vehicles, which may be the way of the future, repair facilities for both trucks and any vehicles belonging to the cooperative and its residents.

A diner or restaurant for transients and residents. We also will need sleeping accommodations for any and all transients, don't forget some recreational facilities, and adequate parking for overnight stays. Total area 400' x 400' broken down appropriately

<u>North East Corner</u> will house the preparatory and storage This is where the packaging and preparatory areas will be constructed of 200' x 400' for preparation and packaging and

200' x 400' for storage facilities. Complete with loading docks and produce unloading bins.

<u>South East Corner</u> of 330' x 400 will house the service facilities of the entire community, including all equipment and power storage for electric power any water supply

<u>South West Corner</u> will house all the offices and areas that service the welfare of the cooperative community including municipal functions - such as peace control, fire control, and all municipal functions

COMMUNITY OPERATIONAL OFFICES

COOPERATIVE OPERATIONAL OFFICES

WEST   FRONT STREET   EAST

WEST   FRONT STREET   EAST

WAREHOUSE

PACKING PLANT

TRUCK STOP

WASH AND PARKING

GAS PUMPS

Main St - The retail stores and public service area set at the southern end of the cooperative. An area of approximately 800' wide and 800' long with enough excess area for growth.

The S.W section of 350' x 400' will hold the bank and the movie theater. The S.E. section of 350' x 400' will hold the super market and the fast food restaurant. The six section will be the medical and service area including a super drugstore and Dr's offices.

The NW section will hold the retail stores and local merchants. These areas will be 350' x 350' each. Down the center will be the main shopping street of the community with adequate parking in each area, for the residents who utilize the area.

At each ends of the street and across the road will be room for growth and further construction.

No traffic lights are planned at this time, but stop signs and yield signs will be enforced.

All businesses will be owned and operated by private individuals, under franchise agreement from the cooperative and will be considered as residents and citizens of entire community. Housing and benefits will be available to all.

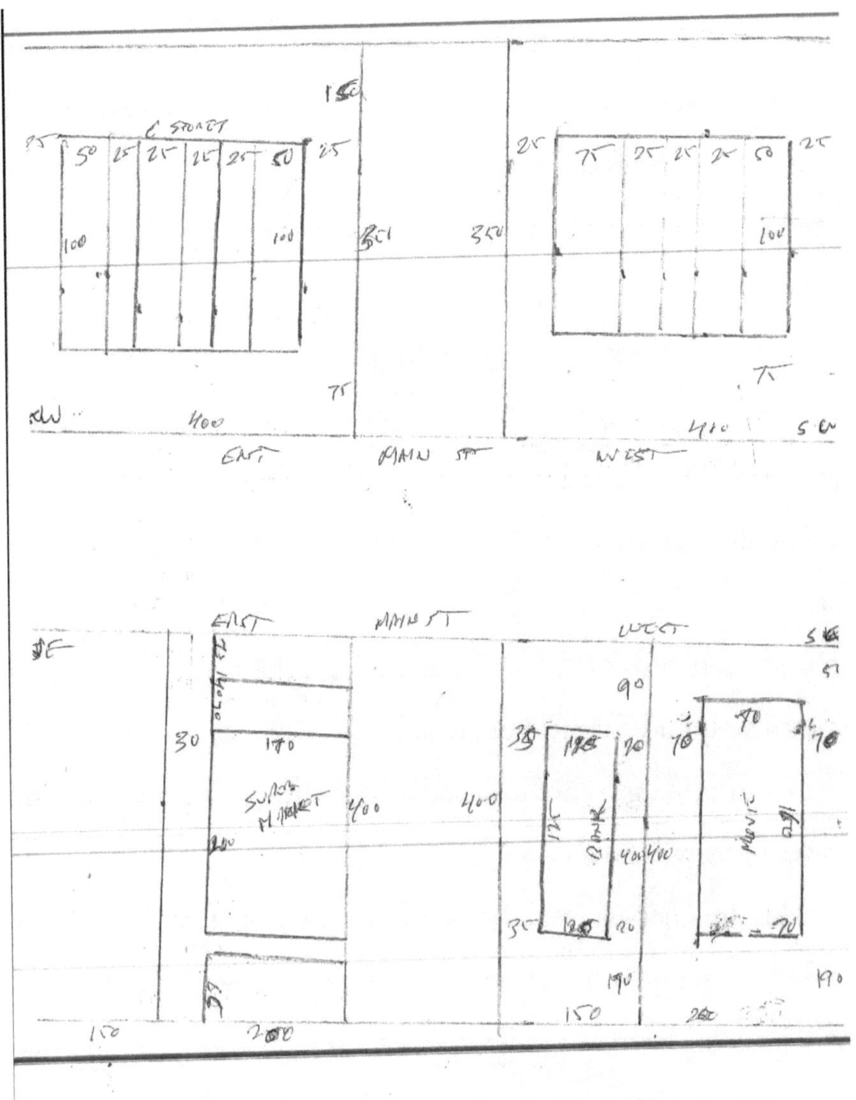
STORE
50 25 25 25 25 50 25
100 100
150
250 350
75
KW 400
EAST MAIN ST WEST
25 75 75 25 25 50 25
100
75
400 50

SE
EAST MAIN ST WEST SE ST
30 90
OLD JAIL
170 35 175 90 70 70 70
SUPER MARKET 400 400 125 BANK 400/400 MONTE 170
200
35 175 20 70
190 190
50 150 250
150 200

Commercial Rental Rates $10 per foot (approx.)

20 x 80	1600' feet	$1600 per mo
25 x 80	2000 feet	$2000 per mo
30 x 80	2400 feet	$2400 per mo
45 x 80	3600 feet	$3600 per mo
90 x 80	7200 feet	$7200 per mo
150 x 150	(approx.) 22,500 ft.	$15,000 per mo
Larger parcels		$5 per foot per mo
Professional suites		$10 per foot per mo (approx.)

30 x 80	½ split	2400 feet	$1200 per mo
20 x 80	Full	1600 feet	$1600 per mo
30 x 80	Full	2400 feet	$2000 per mo
30 x 90	Full	1200 feet	$1,000 per mo
80 x 80	Full	6400 feet	$2,800 per mo
80 x 90	Full	7200 feet	$3000 per mo
400 x 350	Full or Part	16000 ft.	$6500 per mo (approx.)

Other parcels of other size - build yourself

Subject to negotiation and construction costs

All commercial leases are net leases

Renter is responsible for utilities - water electric etc

Garbage disposal and in some cases property taxes

All private leases - Require lessees will pay for all utilities. Plus a community maintenance fee of $200 per month. The same fee applies to all commercial leases also

<u>Traffic Rules</u> - Strictly adhered to

Speed limit - On Main and Front St.	20 mph
On Atlantic and Pacific Avenues	35 mph
On All Section Streets and Roadways	15 mph

For the safety and security of residents and children

Stop sign means stop and then go - not roll thru

Parking in designated parking spots only

No parking in fire lanes & or in front of walkways

Be considerate of the other person's rights and feelings

Violations and discrepancies of cooperative rules can be subject to a fine or other action. By cooperative council review process available by request of regiment.

<u>General Hours of Operation.</u>

Retail Stores - General Products	9:00 am
to 6:00 pm	
Food or Daily Need Stores	8:00 am
to 8:00 pm	
Breakfast/Lunch - 7:00 am to 2:00 pm Dinner	4:00 pm
to 8:00 pm	

Service Facilities - theater - bank etc   As posted

Professional Services Dr's - Lawyers etc   8:00 am

to 4:00 pm

Or by Appointment Not all providers are available every day

Community Mess Hall. Open to all residents and guests

Residents Daily Menu - 3 meals a day $84 per week

Individual Meals (Guest only)	Breakfast	$4.00
(Per Person - all ages)	Lunch	$7.50
(Over 2 yrs. of age)	Dinner	$10.00

Guided Walking Tour of Cooperative (Up to 3 hours total)

9:00 am including breakfast	$7.50
Children 6 yrs. thru 12 years and seniors	$5.00
Children under 6 yrs	N/C
12:00 pm including lunch	$9.50
Children 6 yrs. than 12 years and seniors	$7.00
4:00 pm including diner	$12.50
Children 6 years thru 12 years and seniors	$10.00
Walking tour without meal	$3.50

Community Mess Hall - Open to all (Buffet Style)

Breakfast   6:00 am to 10:00 am (all inclusive) $4.00

Lunch   11:00 am to 2:00 pm (all inclusive) $7.00

Dinner   4:00 pm to 8:00 pm (all inclusive) $10.00

7 days per week - including holidays -

All patrons are requested to leave their seat clean and put their tray and utensils on dish rack on the way out. Show consideration for next persons

Pool Rules For the benefit and safety of all

No running - diving - horse play in the pool area

No diapers of any kind in the pool itself

No children under in pool alone. Must be supervised

No children under 3 in pool at all. Must be toilet trained

Bring your own towels and use them to sit on

Clean up after yourself - wipe down chairs and lounges

Put all trash in proper containers - clean up

No lifeguard on duty - swim at your own risk

Organic Products - Fields and Rotation

There will be 4 field of 3000' long and 4000' wide

Each field be surrounding the main compound with room for expansion.

Each field will yield 2 crops at the same time with 2 plantings, spring and fall

5 type of crops will be assigned to each field for the purpose of rotating the crop fields

(Examples)

South East Field	North East Field
Cucumbers	Zucchini
Artichokes	Spinach
Beets	Brussel Spouts
Carrots	Arugula
Radishes	Peppers

South West Field	North West Field
Cabbage	Celery
Cauliflower	Corn
Lettuce	String beans
Squash	Onions
Leeks	Eggplant

Plus any other product that would fit in the rotation. The field will be tended by 8 permanent personel all year long, Additional personel will be hired for planting and harvesting.

(N) ↑

3000' FIELDS

ATLANTIC AVE

MAPLE CIRCLE

CHERRY CIRCLE

PT AND GYM   POOL

MAIN ST

GYM HALL

CENTRAL WATERWAY

APPLE CIRCLE

ORANGE CIRCLE

MAIN ST

PROFESSIONAL CHURCH

PACIFIC AVE

2000' FIELDS

EPILOGUE

It would be beneficial to interview experts in urban farming, community farming, organic farming to bring in a variety of ideas that would propel this community development into reality and supply a list of resources for organic farming.

About the Author

Kerry Freeman

I am now 85 years old, and I started my writing career at age 75. Over the last 10 years, I have published 8 books, all of which were ideas conceived in a dream. For me, I am not seeking glory nor riches. I am more concentrating on accomplishment. Perhaps some of my thoughts can make things better for others. Hope my fiction mystery novels give enjoyment to my readers.

I will always be glad to discuss my ideas with anyone, who is interested at "mr.kings@aol.com"

Contributor

Robbin "Rivka" Freeman

Robbin is a NYS licensed registered pharmacist and a clinical nutritionist for 35 years. At age 26, starting at the beginning of her oldest child's pregnancy, she exhibited breast cancer symptoms. She was officially diagnosed with breast cancer 22 months later. After 13 breast surgeries, she started eating organic in order to recover and manage relapses; and now living 34 years later by eating whole food plant based no oils dist.

Robbin can be reached at <u>Nutriph@live.com</u>.

www.ingramcontent.com/pod-product-compliance
Lightning Source LLC
Chambersburg PA
CBHW051424250726
48655CB00003B/1224